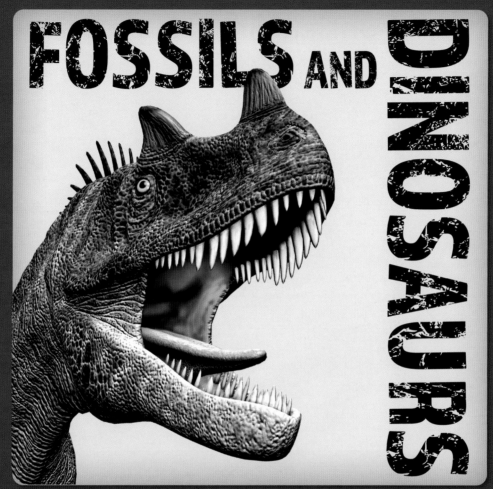

FOSSILS AND DINOSAURS

by Julie K. Lundgren

A Crabtree Seedlings Book

CRABTREE
Publishing Company
www.crabtreebooks.com

T0021051

Paleontology (pay-lee-uhn-TOL-uh-jee):
the study of ancient life using fossils

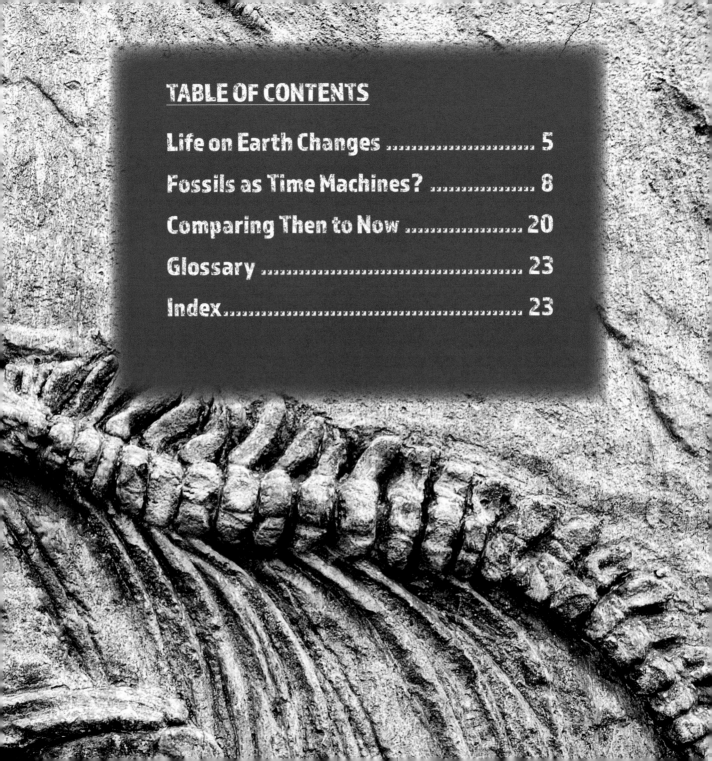

TABLE OF CONTENTS

Life on Earth Changes

Life on Earth has changed over time. Today's plants and animals differ from the past. Flowers and furry animals, such as dogs, cats, and rabbits, came much later in Earth's history.

dinosaurs
(DYE-nuh-sorz)

Some life-forms, such as **dinosaurs**, no longer exist. Dinosaurs once lived on every **continent** on Earth.

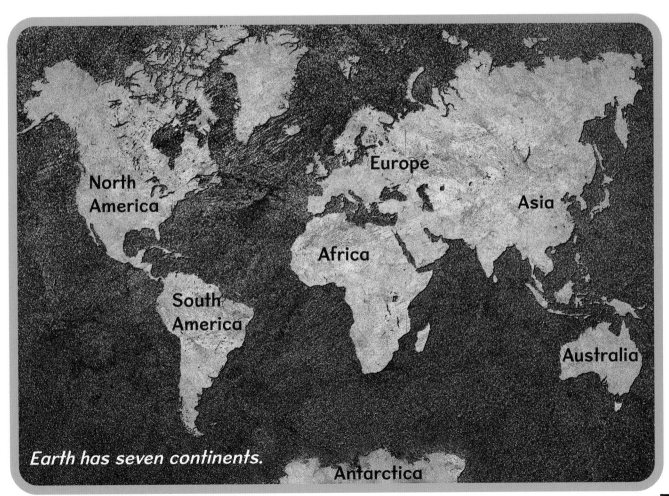

North America

Europe

Asia

Africa

South America

Australia

Earth has seven continents.

Antarctica

Fossils as Time Machines?

We learn about **prehistoric** life on Earth through **fossils**. By studying fossils, we can look back through millions of years.

dragonfly fossil

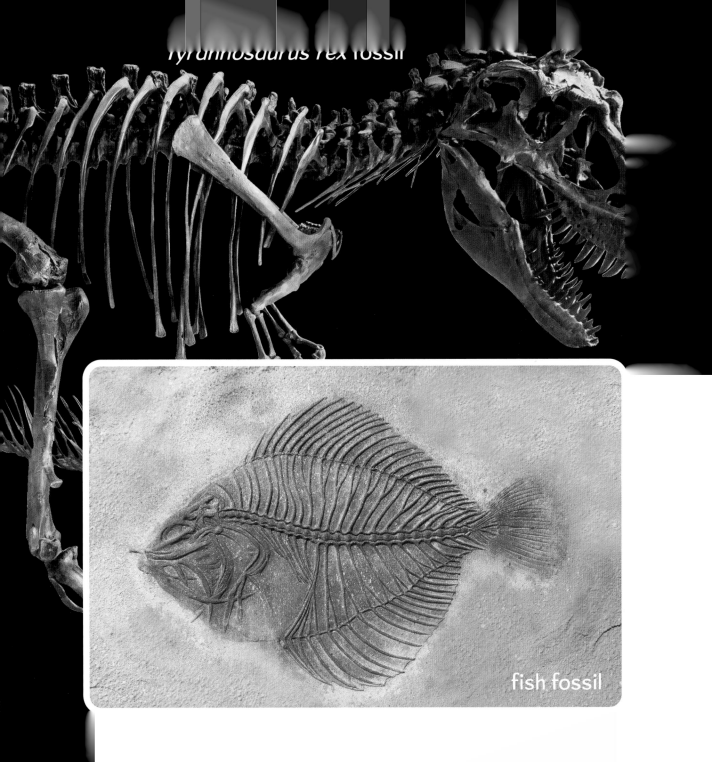

Tyrannosaurus rex fossil

fish fossil

Paleontologists have uncovered fossils of dinosaur bones, teeth, feathers, scales, claws, eggs, nests, and footprints.

teeth

eggs

claw

footprint

Paleontologists can measure the age of fossils and learn which dinosaurs lived at the same time.

Paleontologists use rock layers to learn the age of fossils. The oldest fossils are on the lower layers and the newest fossils are on the upper layers.

From the shape, size, and contents of fossil eggs, we can learn what kind of dinosaur laid them.

By studying plant and dinosaur fossils from the same age and area, we can begin to understand dinosaur life and **habitats**.

Footprints provide clues about how fast a dinosaur moved and if it walked on two or four feet.

Allosaurus, *a meat-eater, and* Brachiosaurus, *a plant-eater, lived about 140 million years ago.*

Allosaurus
(al-uh-SOR-uhs)

Dinosaurs lived between 245 million and 65 million years ago.

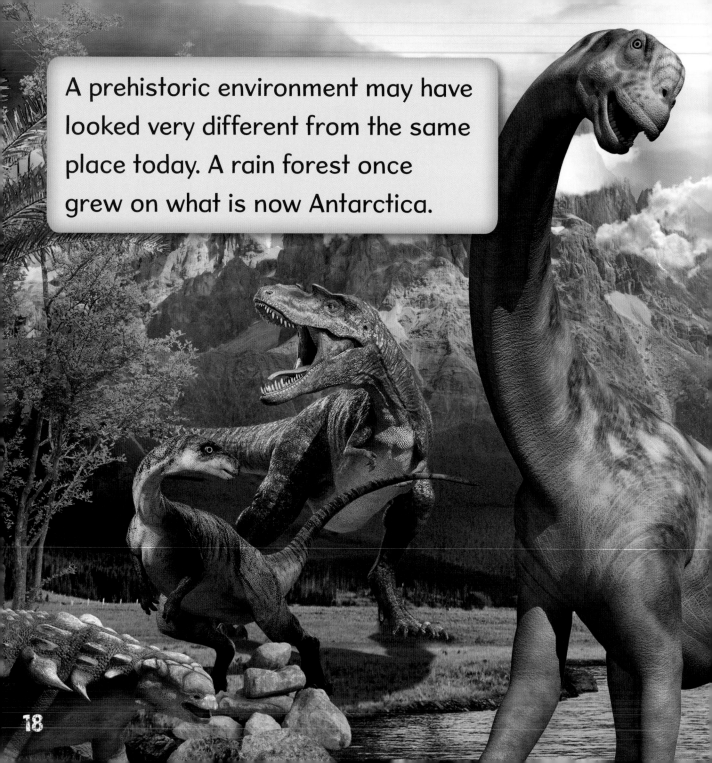

A prehistoric environment may have looked very different from the same place today. A rain forest once grew on what is now Antarctica.

Antarctica today

Comparing Then to Now

We can **compare** dinosaur fossils to each other, and to animals today. Clues from fossils point to birds as the closest living relatives of dinosaurs.

Velociraptors *had feathers and hollow bones like birds.*

Velociraptor
(vuh-LOSS-uh-RAP-tur)

roadrunner
(ROHD-ruhn-ur)

As we dig and study more fossils, we will learn more. Exciting discoveries are still to be found.

Glossary

compare (kuhm-PAIR): To judge one thing against another and notice similarities and differences

continent (KON-tuh-nuhnt): One of the seven large land masses on Earth

dinosaurs (DYE-nuh-sorz): A large group of reptiles that lived on Earth in prehistoric times

fossils (FOSS-uhlz): The remains of animals and plants from long ago, preserved in rock

habitats (HAB-uh-tats): Places where plants and animals naturally live

paleontologists (pay-lee-uhn-TOL-uh-jists): Scientists who study fossils

prehistoric (pree-hi-STOR-ik): Belonging to a time before history was recorded in written form

Index

School-to-Home Support for Caregivers and Teachers

This book helps children grow by letting them practice reading. Here are a few guiding questions to help the reader build his or her comprehension skills. Possible answers appear here in red.

Before Reading

- **What do I think this book is about?** I think this book is about dinosaurs and where they lived. I think this book is about why dinosaurs no longer exist.

- **What do I want to learn about this topic?** I want to learn more about what dinosaurs ate. I want to learn if dinosaur skeletons in museums are the real bones of dinosaurs.

During Reading

- **I wonder why...** I wonder why there are dinosaur eggs that never hatched. I wonder why a rain forest once grew on Antarctica and why it's now covered with snow.

- **What have I learned so far?** I have learned the birds of today are the closest living relatives of dinosaurs. I have learned that *Velociraptors* had feathers and hollow bones like the birds of today.

After Reading

- **What details did I learn about this topic?** I have learned that paleontologists are scientists who study fossils. I have learned that some dinosaurs had claws and very sharp teeth.

- **Read the book again and look for the glossary words.** I see the word *dinosaurs* on page 7, and the word *prehistoric* on page 8. The other glossary words are found on page 23.

Library and Archives Canada Cataloguing in Publication

CIP available at Library and Archives Canada

Library of Congress Cataloging-in-Publication Data

CIP available at Library of Congress

Crabtree Publishing Company
www.crabtreebooks.com   1–800–387–7650

Written by: Julie K. Lundgren

Production coordinator and Prepress technician: Tammy McGarr

Print coordinator: Katherine Berti

Print book version produced jointly with Blue Door Education in 2022

Printed in the U.S.A./CG20210915/012022

PHOTO CREDITS:
istock.com, shutterstock.com, Cover; Bob Orsillo. PG2-3 and back cover: 501room. PG4-5: absolutimages, para827. PG6-7:Allexxandar, Herschel Hoffmeyer. PG8-9: stockdevil, mirecca, aodaodaod. PG10-11: dgero, neenawat, MarcoCavina, paleontologist natural. PG12: Pino62 | Wickimedia https://creativecommons.org/licenses/by-sa/3.0/deed.en, PG 13 Daniel Indiana. PG14-15: Elnur, LuFeeTheBear, markrhiggins. PG16-17: Nine_Tomorrows, DARREN HOOK. PG18-19: Photodynamic, AmeliAU. PG20-21: leonello, MikeLane45. PG22: Nils Knötschke, CC BY-SA 2.5 -Generic_https://creativecommons.org/licenses/by-sa/2.5/deed.en.

Published in the United States
Crabtree Publishing
347 Fifth Ave.
Suite 1402-145
New York, NY 10016

Published in Canada
Crabtree Publishing
616 Welland Ave.
St. Catharines, Ontario
L2M 5V6